Address of Paradise

To Krysia, Jerzy and Andrew, Natasha and Ghislain, and the family of Zofia Ilinska, for whom this book was intended.

ADDRESS OF PARADISE

Zofia Ilinska

TABB HOUSE
Padstow

First Published 1996
Tabb House, 7 Church Street, Padstow, Cornwall, PL28 8BG

'When I return to Poland' was first published in *Horoscope of the Moon*, Tabb House, 1992.

The publishers cannot attempt to explain the pronounciation of Polish but point out that the name Tatus is pronounced Tahtoosh.

ISBN 1 873 951 31 0

British Library Cataloguing-in-Publication Data:
a catalogue record of this title is available from the British Library.

Printed by St George Printing Works Ltd, Redruth

CONTENTS

Page

THE ESCAPE

ENVOI

FOREWORD

Address of Paradise is Zofia Ilinska's third collection of poems in English. It is to a large extent the result of a journey she took in 1992 when after more than half a century in exile she returned to the Poland of her childhood. The poems recreate not so much what she found there but what was missing – a past which appeared suddenly as distant and other-worldly as paradise. In lesser hands such a task would have led to something sentimental or overtly personal. But as with her last collection, *Horoscope of the Moon*, Ilinska shows herself to be a poet of rare gifts. She is able to sustain verse which is at once autobiographical and universal, which although essentially elegiac is suffused with joy and wit.

Zofia Ilinska was born in 1921, in that corner of north-eastern Europe known to the Poles as 'Kresy' or the 'borderlands' and now divided between Lithuania and Belarus. Seven years of war and revolution had left this much-trampled swathe of territory in the hands of Poland. Just a year before her birth, Ilinska's parents had moved back to Kresy to find their house at Moryn had been burnt to the ground. Rebuilding it took them two years and when they moved in, with the young Ilinska swaddled amidst a cartload of furniture, the villagers stood and watched. 'Now,' they laughed, 'there'll be something to loot again.'

And so it proved. Sixteen years later, on September 17th, 1939, Ilinska's family fled on the same farmcarts, spent three days dodging the Red Army's advance and crossed into Lithuania with rifle-bullets whining about their ears. For fifty-three years, Ilinska had no idea what had happened to the world she had left behind, the house on the river Niemen, the silver they had buried, the people she knew, the animals. But when the Soviet Union collapsed she was able to return. Like her parents seventy years earlier, she stepped into the village to find that the house had been burnt down.

Address of Paradise is, in part at least, an attempt to understand the baffling distance between her first world and her life in exile. Recurring throughout the cycle is the figure of the 'Word' – indeed this was for a long time one of her working titles, another was simply 'Roots'. The Word here is multi-faceted. It represents the unifying of her dual identities. But it is used also in its Biblical sense, as something that precedes language, that Ilinska was aware of from the cradle, that was jostled and harried by her move from one end of Europe to the other, and appears sometimes in its Polish guise and sometimes in its English. It is also the speech of her conscience chastising her for abandoning her given tongue; and in the end she recognises it as that mysterious fount of internal chatter and song which drives the poet to the page.

When she arrived in England during the war, Ilinska lodged in a convent in Essex. There she learned sufficient English to enrol on a course of English literature at Reading University. On her twenty-first birthday she recalls the anguish she felt at knowing that Byron was already an established poet at her age. But by the end of the war she had published two volumes of poetry in Polish.

In 1946 she married and moved to the village of St Mawes in Cornwall. For thirty years she and her husband ran hotels. They had two children and though her duties kept her too often from her writing, Ilinska was too busy to mind. 'Summer Happiness', a poem from her last collection, *Horoscope of the Moon* is a snapshot of this period:

> Mother, cook, driver, gardener, beachcomber
> Driving down country lanes with flocks of young;
> Surfing boards, picnic-baskets, ice cream, song
> I have not read a poem all the summer
> Or even nibbled at a line of verse . . .

In *Address of Paradise*, Ilinska puts aside her Cornish self to examine the Polish-Slavic core of her identity. As in all her verse there is a playful love of language, words are rolled around and savoured on the tongue; she uses rhyme and metre and revels in forms like sonnets, haikus and rondeaux. As with so many of her generation of poets, her early influence was Eliot (she translated *Murder in the Cathedral* into Polish), but she brings to her second language a lyricism and music that is all her own. Her range of mood and tone is consistently surprising. There are poems in this collection like 'The Roads of Europe' in which a few lines make the facts of history suddenly palpable; others are comic, others metaphysical; many like 'Following Big Bang', which imagines the first emergence of life, are both: 'Helter skelter muddy muddled / The creatures creep out of the cosmic puddle . . .'

By the early eighties Ilinska was writing again in earnest. The circumstances that gave her time also gave her the themes which made up *Horoscope of the Moon*. She was now widowed; her only son had been killed in a car crash and the hotels had been sold to receivers. While the summers were spent in running her house far paying guests, the Cornish winters were put aside for reading and writing. Books arrived regularly in bundles from the London Library. She read widely in Polish, English and French, researching the poems and relishing in particular science, to which she brought the clear, poetic understanding of someone who had never received the slightest scientific schooling.

In 1992, when she was travelling in the post-Soviet strangeness of her homeland, she was astonished to find that there she could write only in Polish. The poem 'Niemen', composed beside the river which had shaped her childhood, appeared to her in Polish – the Word had sprung on her one of its last surprises. In 'Three Graves', she records with nursery rhyme simplicity the looting of her father's grave, and it was this moment – discovering the empty tomb in a damp tangle of forest – that shocked her most of all. On her return to Cornwall she set up a fund to restore the graves and rebuild the village chapel. In June 1994 she returned for its reconsecration and saw the River Niemen for the last time. Shortly after this second journey, she was diagnosed as having cancer; typically she responded by writing the poems that end this collection. She died a year later, in October 1995.

Although writing was never a career, and although she was never involved in the cut-and-thrust of the literary world, Zofia Ilinska was a natural poet and a true poet. She was dedicated to her craft, labouring tirelessly to attain her seamless lines, to draw something universal from her experience. Her life was a rare achievement not because of what she suffered but because it failed to rob her of the bright qualities which come out so clearly in her verse. Her work remains a brilliant fusion of the exotic and the mundane, the profound and the humorous, as much a product of Cornish walks as of fleeing from murderous armies. She was the child of a Europe that has vanished, jettisoned into a world where she never quite lost the freshness of a stranger's eye. This collection is her witness.

Philip Marsden

Also by Zofia Ilinska :

Duch Lorda Curzona
Wichry w Zbóu
Missing
Night in Lamorran (verse play)
Idle Rocks
Horoscope of the Moon

Introduction

THREE DREAMS

Three dreams of childhood constantly recurring: one – wild, prophetic. The second dream very peaceful: an apple.

1. THE ESCAPE

I am the driver of a carriage and a pair of chestnut horses. They are our farm horses. I do not remember their names. My mother and young brothers are with me in the carriage lying on straw. Although in mortal danger and fleeing from some deadly enemy who is close on our heels, I am not scared. I brandish my whip in the air with panache and gusto, the horses gallop, the speed is fantastic. I am marvellous, magnificent, a paragon of courage, heroic, my family's saviour and guardian angel; intoxicated with the power and speed of the horses and the success of the flight. We gallop through a thick forest of pine trees down a rough track of wolf's claw moss (*lycopodium-widlaki*). The rays of the setting sun paint the bark of the pines with dark yellow, orange and red.

The dream was in Polish.

2. THE APPLE

The apple is as huge and round as a water melon.
It is so heavy it is not easy to hold it.
Colour of a flushed cox orange pippin.
It has no name.
It is a very strange apple because there is no flesh in it only Juice. Juice only underneath the rind.

I marvel at the way the rind is able to hold so much liquid and
Yet appear so hard and so firm.
What happens if I make a little hole in the skin of the apple;
Would the juice leak out?
I do not make the hole.
I touch it gently.
It feels mysterious.

The dream was in Polish.

The third dream – very recent – was also prophetic.

3. WHEN I RETURN TO POLAND

When I return to Poland I will find it altered
Moved like a building-block from East to West
Still taming, still adjusting its new map-places.

When I return to Poland after fifty years
Three friends will be there to greet me with gifts of mushrooms
Picked in the Torun forest, and Holy Week palms.
Someone somewhere will say "But you have an accent!"

When I return to Poland I shall be astonished
To hear my native language talked on street corners
Freely – alive and kicking – intelligent – vital;
Astonished to see the fields being ploughed by horses,
Well-cared for, gleaming horses returning from market
With – often – a cow in the *fura* – the long wooden carriage.
Chickens will scratch by the roadside unafraid of traffic;
Churches will burst at the seams and ancient buildings
Restored after bombs will bow and plead for attention.

When I return to Poland I shall be invited
to read my long-age poems in a place of learning.
The room will be full of professors. They will listen, attentive.
In the back of the room, amidst them, Mother Tongue wearing
a robe of mystical gold – liturgical – hieratic –
(I see her always in gold, the Mother of Words)
Her pensive face, the gesture of hand absolving
this Prodigal Daughter who squandered, scattered
her heritage of words in foreign lands.

When I return to Poland an unknown poet
Will offer me yellow freesias. In my Square of Emotion
Two giant horses will stand in the moistened air
On patient powerful feet, high priests of that land,
With pale-pink pompons dancing round their ears;
They will turn their heads towards me, beckoning, laughing
with soft benevolent mouths, curving their lips
in a deep horsy laugh, offering friendship –
The gurgly home-coming laugh . . . I shall stroke and kiss
Their velvet muzzles, their sloping chestnutty cheeks
With darkness around the eyes and weep a little
Smelling the meadows in them, smelling Poland in them.

The dream was in English.

DO YOU REMEMBER, ANDREW?

Sixty Years Later . . .

Do you remember, Andrew, how the wolf
howled in the frozen forest in the dark,
filling us, listening children, with a shiver?
Do you remember eerie booms, as if
something unearthly, other-worldly, broke –
The cracking of the ice upon the river?

Do you remember, Andrew, how you pushed
the largest of broad beans inside your nose
and then the panic when it stuck somewhere?
And how we waited for the beanstalk-bush
to sprout out of your nasal cavities
and doctors' brouhaha and Mama's despair?

Do you remember war and how we fled
with you and Jerzy slumbering in the hay,
the guns we hid and how the horses galloped
on the world's cobblestones, the empty shed
and us all praying there? How far away,
how very far away – war – youth – and Europe!

Africa – Asia – New Guinea – Australia –
Recited pensively like prayer beads
Tropically sloping towards the Equator.
And this is where I come to find you, Andrew,
in monsoon-moaning eucalyptus woods
edged by rain forest and volcanic crater,

With matted impenetrable creepers, trees,
Funnel-web spiders plotting in their covens,
Ticks, leeches, kookaburras, cockatoos,

Snakes brewing venoms in rain-forest ovens,
Bush dancing round its ancient ring-a-roses
murky and wild as aborigines.

And there you'll always stand for all I know
Calling "kur-kur" in the hibiscus yard,
dispensing corn and love, bran and molasses
to guinea fowl, canaries, bitches, horses
while stinging trees and reptiles wait – on guard –
in their green innocence protecting you.

Interlude

The Bread Riots at Poznan, 1956

THE FAIR OF POZNAN

The city sleeps. The Fair is closed
And shrouded stall of every kind.
Nothing stirs here but the flap-flap
Of flag tormented by the wind.
Remote a hissing up the street,
Remote the whistle of the train.
Tyrants in overalls, hooray,
For the air here it stinks of pain!

The various visitors depart
Each to his separate hotel
To taste the vodka and the borsch
And the pike served in Bechamel
Whispering: "Sometimes these Fairs reveal
The gist of things too dark to tell:
Romantic Poland is alive,
It's with the young ones in the cell."

One said: "I sensed as early as the station
The wind of restlessness move up the streets,
The pavements drenched with wounded agitation,
Laid low, laid low the belly and the meats.
One fell right next to me, a loud young buster
Shouting for bread. Then bangs and shouts and screams.
Still 'BREAD' they yelled as in the Pater Noster,
The poor starved beggars with their poor starved dreams.

What is the meaning of this rage,
The vast immense ferocity,
The strong impulse to break away,
The urge and fury to be free?
For could not, could not freedom grow
Like any common asphodel?

Romantic Poland is alive,
It's with the young ones in the cell."

"I watched some dummy foods," another said
"And dummy articles displayed in shops
When I came on them wrapping their first dead
In blood-stained flags. Cats arched upon roof-tops,
Scared cats miauled in the tiles above my head.
The thought came to me: Brag about progress!
You're dead because you've mumbled about bread!
Others dared call 'Panem et Circenses!' "

"O hear it clang and hear it toll
The violent the funereal bell.
And what if Judas changed to John
And Cain the Crooked to Abel!
Why all the talk of brotherhood
By brother giving brother hell?
Romantic Poland is alive
It's with the young ones in the cell."

One shouted: "Blessing to this Fair of Opulence;
This Festival of Breeding; you and you
Who stand for Peoples' Cause and Common Sense;
Peace. Power. Blackmaggot Earth. Swinefat and glue!
I promise you the world amidst the flags;
I bless you, Comrades; you and you and you."
Two little children in calico rags
Smiled up the stalls: "Mama, and is it true?"

The various visitors depart
Each to his separate hotel
To taste the vodka and the borsch
And the pike served in Bechamel
Whispering: "Sometimes these Fairs reveal

The gist of things too dark to tell:
Romantic Poland is alive.
It's with the young ones in the cell."

A YOUTH OF POZNAN

He worked through the night. Had no sleep.
And again – dawn to dusk. Did not weep.
They gave him a thousand – all coins.
Not enough. Hunger. Belly and loins.
He went marching. Protest. Calling: "Bread."
They shot. He was young. He is dead.

I ask: would he rise if he could,
Tear open his buttons of lead,
Past the criss-cross construction of wood
To go marching again for his bread,
Or remain with the heroes, elect
Where martyrs and saints intercede
And the pleading that's done is direct
Without obligation to bleed?

My First World

I PICK MY NEWBORN WORD

'Like lovers words go strolling
in the vast white park of the book'.
Edmond Jabes

I pick my newborn word in the flat, north–eastern,
overgrown, war-torn patch of a Polish garden.
It gives out chestnut gleams.
The word is Slavonic.
Together we reach towards Mother:
me – me – me –
then quick quick quick towards Father:
tia – tia – tia –
Mamusia – Tatus –
my first dictionaries.

It runs towards me hurriedly adjusting
its pelerine of consonants and vowels
its cargo of prefixes, prepositions
definite articles etc. etc.
I top and tail it like a gooseberry.
It flows down to my pen with astonishing obedience.
The WORD – my very own – allotted – baffling –
nobody else's darling – my little dumpling –
travelling light. From where?
The Babel Towers?
I do not have an idea from where it emerges
or where it roosts amidst the silences.
Cave of the mouth and throat? A moist habitation.
The brain? Some murky nook in which to curl up
between the cortex and the hypothalamus?

Cocoons of emptiness? Some vacant cocoon?
Is that the house of the Word, where the Word waits?
A child of earth and blood? The night and the stars?
Why so inscrutable? Hallowed? Other-wordly?

"Adopted by the human family
I have kept my own rules, defied gravity"
- says the Word.

"Call me a tool, a tool for communication.
To make thought palpable, this is my mission."

I SET OUT BAREFOOT INTO THE CORNFIELDS

So in the visionary company of the Word
I set out barefoot into the cornfields
to rattle in the stubble of my first world,
my patch of paradise on the river Niemen
curing its grey-green body underneath the martins
quick darting in and out of the yellow sandbanks;
close to the piggery, the cow-stables, the low building where
rotund cheeses mature in cells of darkness;
close to the landing stage with the tied-up paddle-boat
and the uncobbled yard where ducks, turkeys, chicken
scratch in the scattered cow-dung and horse-piss straw.

A calf is born this morning
Drops from his mother
The little astronaut
Dances out of birth-trappings
With an artist's finesse
No trouble finding the udder.

I too am learning to milk
Crouching on a stool
Udders smoother than silk
Liquid from the back of beyond
Mysterious as
The curdling of milk.

The dogs are reading my thoughts
We pick prints in the sand
Horse-hoof – cow-hoof – magpie –
Ladybird on the back of my hand
Will you stay?
Will you fly away?

Come,
Let us play with the echo.
My brothers and I
Shout a question, then wait
For the echo's reply:*

Who is the woman most sweet?
Echo answers:
The one you beat.
Who stole from the Tree of Life?
Echo answers:
Wife – wife – wife –

Two storks caress one another
With tender beaks
Kle – kle – kle – kle – kle –
On their straggly nest
I practice the sound
Can it be true that they bring us babies?
I would like to be so caressed
When I grow up.

Bird, pilgrim bird on a branch,
Bird of passage, grey bird,
Perching bird
Kle – kle – kle –
Tioch – tioch – tioch –
Ness – ness – ness –
Imitate all sound –
Says the Word.

* Która najlepsza kobita? Bita.
Kto zjadł jabłko z drzewa? Ewa.

THE RIVER AT THE HOUR OF NOON-TIME MILKING AND THE HORSES

Centuries-old contemplative and silent
The river flows between meadows like a slow movement
Aorting through my heart into the Baltic.

A horse is led to the bank, bends his head and drinks.
The horse, the man with the horse, gaze long into water.
Slow shallow gulping. Immobility.
The cows have gone to pasture, the black and white
  Friesians.
The bees have flown to pasture – daughters, grand-daughters
Of the wild mother bee the Queen, who – while swarming –
Was hijacked by my mother from a broken tree-trunk.
The hives are whitewashed. Seven. Underneath the apple
  trees,
Our seven heavenly shrines in haloes of humming.

The sun is high. The hour of noon-time milking.
The milking women clamber into carts,
Plump meadow-women hitching up long skirts,
Adjusting kerchiefs, driven to cowslip meadows.
"Praised be the Lord Jesus Christ" – each one intones.
"For ever and ever amen" – I answer each.
Vats, buckets, stools are loaded into carts,
The horses wait – one grey, one chestnut, two sorrels.
Siwak, the gelding, has achieved distinction
Swimming the river, his short grey mane dry.

There's no one in the world more patient than
A working horse, his gentle humility,
Ancient, unquestioning benevolence.

The wind plays in his mane which hangs uncombed.
I give them lumps of sugar. They crunch, they whip
Their long dark tails against flies, they wrinkle their skins
Now and then lifting up a sandalled hoof
Ready to tread the sands of those difficult roads.
Oh they are priceless, precious, our reigning princes.
There were no horses here when I was born
Not one single living horse in the entire land.
Gradually one by one brought from the West
In cargo trains on straw from Warsaw to Lida,
Unbelievably precious cargo, accompanied by Tatus.

NIEMEN

Siedzę nad Niemnem i patrzę na łodzie
Kraczą koło mnie jakieś wronie dzieci
Tu słowik śpiewa – tu rybitwa leci;
Wiosło rybaka zanurza się w wodzie.

Te same łąki i te same lasy
Co lata temu – nieme zachwycenie
I dziwna smętna żałość i zdumienie.
Co się z tą wodą stało i z tym czasem?

Chlupocze rzeka : zastanów się siostro
Niemunas – Niemen – czy nie wszystko jedno
Płytka – głęboka – wirująca – ostra

Urokliwa – skupiona – deszczów pełna
Łaskocząc swoje gwiazdy i szczupaki
Do morza pędzę, bo mam rozkaz taki.

*

I sit by the Niemen and look at the boats
Crows' children are cawing around me
Here a nightingale sings – there a tern flies by
A fisherman's oar dips in the water.

The same woods and the same meadows
As years ago – wordless enchantment
And strange, melancholy sadness and surprise.
Where did all the water and the time go?

The river murmurs: ponder this, sister
Nimunas – Niemen – are they not the same?
Shallow – deep – eddying – still

Spell-binding – self-absorbed – in full flood
Tickling my stars and my fish
I rush to the sea, as this is my destiny.

DANCE OF A HUNDRED TAILS

The Moon will dance tonight to the initiated.
The Strays of the land are the first to hear the summons.
Lifting the vagabond leg they leap ahead
Joined by the Dogs of the House, the Dogs of the Farmyard.
With frenzied moonward bows, night eyes aglitter
The company of dogs streaks out in full cry,
Top of their canine shriek, their barking potential,
Streak out, the dogs streak out on urgent paws
To keep the tryst, the pre-ordained assignment.
At breakneck speed, over the ditches, fence,
Past stables, barns, the ice-house,
The startled night-watchman.

Listen, a shrill new chord has been let off
Its chain of heavenly silence,
Let out of its kennel;
More baying strays, the Moryn-Village dogs
Have picked the Moon's electrifying signal.
The dogs streak out, the Moryn dogs streak out
And now the distant Krzywicze, the Belorussian
Hamlet of meadows, oaks – joins up with the clamorous
Hoarse, raucous, weird chorus of canine wailing.

Savage fortissimos, the rare sotto voce,
The mongrel baritone, the bitch soprano.
Ritualistic – savage – ceremonial –
Ordering the worshippers to congregate
Close to the River – deep and shallow – where
The Moon will dance – and where the River offers
A lit up shimmering floor for the Pas de Deux . . .

O magic midnight, maddening exhalations
Of air – water – earth – while regal, enchanting

And amorously entwined they dance – the two
Full – oh so golden Moons – the River-Moon
And the heavenly Moon-of-the-Sky –
Their watery, solemn, sensual, celestial tango,
Veils interstellar blowing crazily
Across their lunar cheeks, their planetary faces;
with meadows humming, night birds ululating,
Spinster star clapping and – on the river bank –
The Dogs – on festive protocolled paws – performing
The syncopated Dance of the Hundred Tails.

ROOTS

Someone has planted a larch in the centre of the lawn
Slender – perpetual – tapering –
Pagan – elemental –
Wrapped in light
So playful that
The River Wind blows in
To windily cavort in the tilting branches
Joined by the Buckwheat Wind
The Forest Wind
And the manury scented
Wind of the Stable-Yards
Creating frolic in the pale-green leafage
Wrinkling the reddish-purple female flowers.

I touch the bark. No resin.
Too young. Unwounded.
Invisible the roots: the larch's, mine.
But oh, how firmly anchored in brackish soil,
the nut-brown belly of Slavonic Europe;
They grope and push and search
for nourishment
and stretch deciphering
the thoughts of the earth,
never forgetting to lay down in rings
of woody circular grain the passing years.

We are the Roots. We sing in underground voices
a Song of Life. We sing the Tree into being.
Light we are. Lucid. Earth-coloured. Secretive.
Tenacious cauldrons of activity.

Our thrust is preordained underneath the surface.
We grope for vision, even under gravestones.
Sometimes we cry in the dark for lack of water.
But not for long: a thousand little root-hairs
are here detecting the approach of juices,
the itch, the tensions of humidity.
Oho – we cry – oho – and spring to attention
to sip the liquid drops as they step down.

We drain the cruder solutions always searching
finer filtrations, fibres, ancient salts,
assembling the vital ingredients,
picking the constant,
casting out the unstable,
dissolving, dissolving,
weighing up, mixing moisture with the air,
always aware of little insistent shrieks
of carbon, sugar, cambium, hydrogen, resin . . .

We work in unison plotting, combining
cell-sap – primeval mud – minerals – magic –
aiming at inevitability.
Earth – although neutral –
gives us dark advice.

THE HOUSE

I struggle with memory.
"Be precise" – says the Word –
"Detail these twitterings from your feudal perch.
Home is whatever lullabies and shelters
The first millimetres of sleep
In your inch-long life.
Home is what you remember."

The house, the lair,
The nest, the rookery, the fox's hole.
I must have dug it out of the unploughed earth
So firmly entrenched it is in soil, swamp, sand
promising permanence, offering bliss,
Showering me with loyalty and goodness.
Oh I would strap it tightly to my back
And carry it forever like a snail . . . .

The slender larch keeps watch on the circular lawn.
Sometimes at dusk I see it fling out its arms
Towards the candle-light inside the House
And every time it happens, the House takes on
An eerie watchful look – listening, waiting
While every object inside it springs to attention:
The samovar, the wolf-skins, the shawl from Venice.

I am not able to decode the message.
Totally wrapped in greenness the House dismisses
Any attempt by light to penetrate.
Withdrawn and full of shadow, darkish, austere,
Partly submerged and like a submarine
It throbs with the violent pulse of unseen currents,
Deep river stuff whirlpooling through the rooms.

Destroyed – rebuilt – adored like nothing on earth.
Low – wooden – painted white – tower at each end.
Virginia creeper slung over the left shoulder.
Memory deep in beds of hollyhocks.
Dark narrow staircase to the haunted attic.
My father's gun in the hall – cartridges – boots –
The dining room: the samovar lives here.
The floors are dark – painted a nutty brown –
My parents' rooms lead out to a dark verandah
(They sleep in separate rooms.) The drawing-room:
Low chairs – flowery chintzes – wolf skins on walls –
This is the room where the ghost plays the piano.
The childrens' rooms look out on the vegetable garden
The avenue of lime trees, the road to the river.

The loo's a humble place down a dark passage
Constructed high over a deep abyss
An elevation like a royal throne
Inviting spells of siesta and meditation
Uncles and aunts have panicked searching for it.
High stoves of coloured tiles reside in each room.
The colour? The size of the logs? Who brings them?
Olga?

Smells – footsteps – creaking floors – doors banging –
  voices –
The smoke of juniper – pine needles – honey –
Lilac – lime flower – resin – smoke of wood –
Sometimes the odour of potato *bliny*,
Fried onion – bacon *skwarki* – burning butter –
And stronger fiercer smells from the kitchen quarters
Dry dog – wet dog – hot sun – tobacco plant –
Or common grass awaking after rain.
The winter smell? Why can I not remember?

THE FOREST

The forest is everywhere – forest and swamp.
It is so close to the House, that often at night I hear the
Forest creatures sharpening claws,
Scratching the moss with their paws
Rocking their babies.
The bolder trees step out,
Peer into windows.
I show them my leafless life.
But now it is late
And as I drift into sleep
A far-off, weird,
Bloodcurdling, mournful sound takes over the night.
I open the *lufcik* –
The little square part of the double-glazed window –
Cold air blows in and with it the howl of the wolf
Baying his private version of the Psalms of David,
Distant lupine lament.

But why do I fear it?
I imagine him there in his furry splendour,
Midnight around his waist,
Lonelier than the angels,
The shaman of the forest
On his throne of pine needles,
Wheat-coloured innocent expelled from nowhere
Need he lament at all?
Is he worshipping, praising,
Thanksgiving for the fat of lambs and hares,
Freedom to hunt in the primeval *puszcza*.
Full of *Widłaki*, wolf-claw and lycopodium?

"C'est le ton qui fait la chanson"
- admonishes the Word.

Detect the tenderness
In the inflections of howling.

The moon is low
Tangled with the branches of poplars.
In the acacia owls begin recitations.
The House lies quiet around me.
We breathe, inhale
The pastoral reeks,
The scents on the late night wind.
The moonlit vastness of horizons.

What can I do with this immensity?

SNOW

You are obsessed with greenness – says the Word.
Greenness is but another ritual.
Observe how snow at one fell swoop dispels
The green hallucinations of the house.

Hares, foxes, heathercocks leave fingerprints
Upon the powdery blank page of snow.
The river's paralysed and gone to ice.
Sleep green, sleep green green grass. No need to grow.

The arctic silences. Snow muffles sound
On icy tiptoes moving like a thief.
Here are the rivers and here are the roads
Where History's headhunters come to grief.

ROAD TO THE RIVER

The dread, the awful dread on the road to the river
Was it connected with goats and the sound of coughing,
the way tobacco plants and cowpat and resin
combined to charm, assault and refuel fear,
with spectral bleatings, bats and the nightbird hooting
at the back of the granary and the haunted crossroads?

Could it have been the river? Its merciless steely
slow immemorial pushing of corpses from Russia?
Their splashless progress, their last unrecorded swim?

Could it have been collisions of past and future?
There are such timeless times when time gets muddled up
and ancestors long dead, former fathers and mothers,
carriers of powerful genes – shriek out from the ruins
of the ways they have lived and died – to remind and
  warn us?

Look, we have no idea what the future's brewing.
Where were these howls, these shots, these aromas of burning?
What strange fermentations of blood rising up with the sap?

Always the road to the river, the sorrowful voices
in the wind, in the leaf, in the moon
The effacing of landmarks.

MY FATHER

My father was a hunter. My father was a lawyer.
My father served in the Polish Uhlans
blown to high heaven by world-war tanks.
My father owned: marsh, forest, sand,
grazing meadow, river-land,
pine acre, corn acre, silver-birch-wolf acre
in the North-Eastern – free at last
for two decades – border country.

My father judged five days of the week
in Jewish, provincial cobblestone Iwje.
There he slept in a humble hotel.
My mother was lonely.
Back to the House he travelled on Friday night
bringing a cartful of loaves enormous as bolsters,
wholemeal and made of rye with caraway seed.
My father's weekends were spent paying the wages,
rebuilding the ruined estate and loving my mother.

His greatest passion was shooting.
One day by mistake
He hit Elka, beloved retriever,
Wept like a beaver.
The aged bitch survived. They hunted together
stalking the swamp and the forest.
They may still be at it.

He put a red cross on my heels when I was born
in case I was muddled with other babies.
When I was eight or nine he began to take me
on hunting expeditions. We tracked wolves and hares
in raptures of reek of fox, mysterious
patterns of paws in snow, worlds of feather and fur.

I was his bold retriever, he was proud of his daughter.
We drove in fat *linijka*'s (one horse carriages)
singing and bumping over roots. We waited
for murmurous flights of birds, wild duck and snipe.
Mosquitoes sang in the bushes. The birds appeared
when it was nearly dark. Their sudden, amazing
smooth, silent, hardly visible streaking above us.
At other times we crept together at dawn
to hear the capercaillie who is deaf when he sings.

His name was Alexander. I called him 'Tatus'.
He called me 'Cipa', a language reserved for hens.
He died of a heart attack at forty four
Just before World War Two.
Virtuti Militari was laid on his coffin.

Aunt Ancia said to my mother:
"One day you'll be grateful
he had the death he had."

And she was right.

THE ADDRESS OF PARADISE

My eyes are full of field and full of cattle,
I hang around barns and beasts nibbling at corn,
Poking at puddles, smelling the harness shed,
Thrilled by a freckled egg-shell,
The half-smile of a cat,
A four-leaved clover, thistle, dandelion,
My never-cut grass of astonishment.

Strange how the barns, the granaries, the stables
Cluster around the well like bars of music,
Rectangles, squares composed around the well,
Always the search for pattern, repetition.
Only the sky is shapeless,
The sky and the forest.
My face is shapeless as I peer down the well,
Its awful, messy, moist, bottomless, lidless
Back-at-me-staring eye of something trapped.
Trapped sky? Trapped water? with
Buckets on ropes
Forever crashing, crashing, crashing
Into it,
My face inside it paler than the air!
Who can I be? But who?
But who can I be?

I shall not be torn from the well
When listen, listen,
Sheltering, bossy, governessy voices
Float in from the side of the House:
Zosia – Zosia –
Each of the lime trees joins
In shouting my name.

This is the answer then:
I am Zosia of Moryn,
Zosia Moryńska, *Panienka*,
The eldest daughter,
Bred on the milk of a goat,
Because none other,
Polish. A baptised Christian,
Girl with the pigtails.
My father calls me 'Cipa'
'My little pullet'
'The Giggler' – to my brothers – and
When less friendly –
'The eldest Daughter of the King of Fat.'
My home: the Manor – Dwó –
Near Iwje – Lida –
County of Nowogrodek –
Kresy – Poland –
Address of Paradise
in the entre deux guerres.

STORM

A heat wave. Red hot heat. Sky trawls a darkness.
The air is sultry, still and weighs like lead.
The frog holds back his croak, the bird his song.
A deadly silence – ominous and total.
The lightning whips the sky.
Death under trees
With the approaching growlings of the god.

In the long lime-tree-rounded house, my father
opens the missal and to all the gathered
family and householders reads the Gospel:
St John's 'In the beginning was the Word . . .'
Then, with the open Missal, having blessed
each corner of the room and of the world,
he leaves the open Missal like a shield
to challenge thunder and the thunderbolt.

Released – the Word steps out to pacify
the amber god of electricity.

GRANDMOTHER

"What is the difference between boys and girls?"
"The boys have broader backs" – answered Grandmother –
"I wish you would not ask idiotic questions."

"But is it really true that storks bring babies?"
"Of course it is not true. Old peasant women
sell babies in the Village on the black market
for twenty zlotys each or some such price."

"The woe that is in sex" – lamented Grandmother.
"I wish one could beget without this nonsense."

She went to her martyrdom in long-sleeved nightgowns,
high-necked and lust-proof vestments of chastity
hand-sewn by nuns, distressed young women and orphans.
Shock briefly blinded her during her first pregnancy.

She was an heiress. Grandfather was handsome.
He wept so much on the eve of their wedding
that Vilia broke its banks and overflowed.

GUIDELINES

Out of the mouths of babes
Books – trees – caves – grottoes –
The spells of heatwave
And the howling gale
I've spun for your amusement
Strings of mottoes . . .

Do not pinch lilacs, lovely-one
And never never trust a man.

Bons comptes – bons amis.

It's your dog's duty
To die for God and country
Respect your parents
Honour their old age.

Money hardens the heart
And that is sure.
10% at least
Must go to the poor.

He is so healthy
Because he's never sorry
For anybody.

Work on your character
Examine your conscience
Each day remember to pray
Be faithful to the earth
Don't be too serious
Dance in the time of dancing
Surtout pas trop de zèle!

You are God's image. It is your duty
To cherish and protect your beauty.
Never scowl and never frown
Try not to mix dark blue with brown.
Spread your radiance, gleam and shine
Be happy, think yourself divine.
Life is fiddlesticks unless
You aim – no less – at holiness.

Above – the angels.
Below – a dog:
Safe you are
As a bug in a rug.

I drink to those who love me well
And all the others go to hell!

Always polite and never late
Keep your nails clean and your back straight
Help older persons with their coats
Whenever queasy gargle your throats
Eat up whatever's on your plate
Try to resist indecent thoughts
And never never masturbate.

There's nothing worse
Than thoughts of darkness.
They are even worse
Than indecent thoughts.

La politesse c'est la courtoisie du coeur.

Centuries of wisdom have taught that sex
Is a mechanism to be regulated
For the purposes of procreation.

Otherwise – 'though often thrilling' –
An incredible waste of time and energy.

Tears toil and trouble begin
When you fall into mortal sin
Angels weep and devils shout
It is not easy to climb out.

By dressing modestly you'll assuage
The masculine libido's lust and rage.

God is a wild elusive fox
Much easier hunted in a pack.

Do not be too sweet
Or you will be licked to death.

Remember that your ancestors
Died so that you may live in peace.
Reward them with a life
Worthy of their deaths.

An unexamined life
Is not worth living.

SNAKE

I saw a snake. My heart stood still –
The sleek and savage streak.
He slunk away. I could have killed,
Yet feared. He seemed so evil.

I wondered if my wish to kill
And the primeval fear
Were not as deadly as the stock
Of poison he had brewed.

We each held back our stab of death.
Politely, with distaste
Slithered away our separate ways
A coldness on each face.

VIPER IN THE HIVE

The viper's hooked on honey.
Without shaking a drop of dew
It makes its entrance into
The heart of the hive
To worship in
The shrine, the humming hall.

Will bees immediately
Stick with sharp arrows
The thick skin of the reptile,
Or will they wait
Patiently in the wings
And give it time
To suck, sip, lick, adore
The beloved cocktail?

And only when
Quite stupefied by bliss
Stretched out in drunken stupor
Will they strike
Stabbing with stings,
Then mummify in wax
The inert coils
Inside their fitted coffin?

BEES AND POETRY

Some time before my birth
Mother was badly
Stung by wild bees
(a swarm she tried to capture).
The poison almost killed her
causing high fever,
vomiting, lack of breath
and fearful swelling.

Oohoo – oohoo – oohoo –
Lamented the Gipsy.
What will become of the child?
A poet: or worse?

THE RAFT

Yes, yes, I've got a raft – I assure the Word --
The smallest church in the world
Between forest and river
Floating through meadows of burdock and belladonna.
Low – wooden – humble – rustic – no bell to toll,
No ancient stone, no chanted ritual.
A plaster Christ clutching a plaster lamb,
Showering grace upon us,
Wild cherry blossom.

Come, let us enter, kneel before the altar
Among the peasants heads bent low in prayer
Shawled – soil-burnt – solemn
Agricultural faces.
It is the silence of the Consecration.
It is the silence of the elevation,
The whispered sacramental formulae. The priest
Stretches out both host-holding hands so high
That they leap out of the black cassock sleeves
Exposing thin, white human wrists. Conjuring
Alien vibrations from the magic air.
Incomprehensible. Weird. Sacrificial.
Baffling disguises of the Eucharist.

Across the motes of dust, out of the dense
Accumulated heat of psalm, sigh, candle-flame,
Spell, litany, metaphor, invocation,
Mantra, mandala, prayer, incantation
The plaster Christ strikes out,
The luminous panther,
Like a discharge of electricity,
A flash of lightning,
Energy not spilling
Into the orbits of the Bread of Heaven.

The priest now lowers the Host,
He's the lightning conductor,
Insulates it inside the tabernacle,
and on the tongue.
(Another kind of earthing.)

A butterfly, an Admiral, has erred
Into the church, wings beating against glass.
Scent of acacia in the open door.
The clouds are full of lark song. Swallows patrol
Demure in black and white like little nuns.

The Mass is ended. *Ite missa est.*
Go, aim at wholeness, aim at holiness.
I have renewed my youth like that of an eagle.

HOW TO MARK YOUR TERRITORY

"Immensity? Attachment to the soil?"
– Cries the Word austerely –
"I am beating with my little fists
on the doors of your understanding."

When the heart's too bewildered,
too full,
why not join the dawn-chorus
or howl
with the wolf
on the edge of the swamp?

Like the bird, like the wolf you are moved
by an instinct as old as the earth,
tribal urge, territorial belonging,
a decree, a command deeply heard
more insidious than male-female lusting,
more compulsive than call of the herd.

Bird is not permitted to sing,
Stretch wings, build nest, nurture young,
savour the beakful of worms
outside the branch of his preening,
leafy space, stamping ground clearly marked
with the peck of beak,
lick of fur,
ceremonial rolling in muck, scratch of claw,
squirt of urine on bark,
golden urine subtler than ink.

Pick then your landmark
Pick the deeply rooted
never forgotten

long-accustomed places
river – house – poplar –
meaningful – snow-laden –
the path – the swamp –
the cranberry reclining
in her seraglio of moss
like a moody infanta.

They'll scorch the memory, so
gently – gently
pick them with tongs
and hook them to the heart.

Then – if with faith
and passionate awareness
you wish these ancient symbols to endure
melting to lifelong shapes
like the spiral mantles
which mollusc creatures ferry
on sloping shoulders
(invisible loads of beatitude)
then – having picked your landmark –
reverently –
(It is a sacramental occupation)
set out upon your ceremonial walk
bowing your prayerful self
towards the strangely
unfathomable foldings and unfoldings
of landscape, feeling, sound – and
like the beasts of the field
learn to deposit your own mark on each,
a sign – a seal – a cypher –
tangible –
WORD – meaning language –
Sublunary graffiti.

FOLLOWING BIG BANG

Helter skelter muddy muddled
The creatures creep out of the cosmic puddle
On paws hooves bellies fins and feet
Attempting to communicate.
They waggle wet primeval toes
And croak and glare and wrinkle the nose
And grunt and bellow howl and hoot
Cluck cackle twitter screech and bleat
Snarl snort and sneer and shrug and hiss
Preen mate and roll the eyes and kiss
With bow wow wows and quack quack quacks
Little hairs raised on napes of necks
While ululations rise from each:
Oh grant us language! Grant us speech!

Following on Big Bang the Word becomes
Aware of minute, busybody, urgent,
Dynamic entities: neutrons, neutrinos,
Word-souls, echoes of rhythms, waves of impulses
Demanding recognition, so the roots gravely
Went into action: carving signs, lines, hooks
Each one from nothing but a strip of cloud
Selecting for their pattern flights of cranes,
The backs of water turtles, prints of birds' feet.

The Word is thrilled with their intricate carvings.
"Let's call them Characters! Let's call them Letters!"
And just as then Adam is naming the
Breathtaking creatures emerging from Earth,
Likewise the Word – hugging them in his arms –
Gives every newborn shape its appellation.
Whispering "I'll take you down
To the Land of the Living."

And all the time – whether still carving, cutting
Or drying letters wet from the sweat of birth
Word is aware of a Divinity
Eerily haunting in the gap of space
As if some awesome destiny awaited
These deaf-dumb-blind and rodlike Characters.

I don't know what apprenticeship
The Regiment of Letters, those brave little warriors,
Go through before they launch their first attack
Upon the battlefields of the Blank Page.

THE WORD'S CURRICULUM VITAE

My origin? My ancestry?
My pedigree? My habitation?
Unstable, wild, amoral, free
I defy gravity,
Blow cobwebs off reality.
I am a tool.
A tool for communication.

Mystery, mischief up my sleeve
Spells I weave, mountains heave,
From secret sources grace receive.
Bird of Paradise my feathers
Preening, preening . . . Nothing matters
As long as I'm nourished, watered
By my letters.

Though you skin me to the bone
You will not know what makes me tick.
Call me Sorcerer, call me Quack,
Call me the Mask to screen your face
From the scary visage of truth
Peering at you
Through an uncemented crack.

I have learnt to skip and dance
Creep and crawl and roll and rock
One o'clock, two o'clock
Till I get into the trance
Of absolute intelligence
Then perhaps collapse
Into silence?

And it is not my business what
Liturgies, cargoes, substance
The tongue induces for my sake
Be it the sincere milk of goodness,
The deadly venom of the snake,
Or the babblings of the fool.

Communicate. I am the tool.

CALL ME A TOOL – SAYS THE WORD

"Adopted by the human family
I have kept my own rules, defied gravity,"
   – says the Word.

Call me a tool, a tool for communication.
Making thought palpable, this is my mission.
Rootling out truffles of reality.
No-one possesses me. I am wild. I am free.
One instant – fast asleep under the hills,
The next – most active of tools,
Busier than the plough that tills
The brown soil or the weapon that kills, or
The grave-digging spade, or
The hand that fills
Receptacles . . .

Call me a shield for warding off the world's
High-polished surfaces, for I have learned
To curl inside a voice and neutralise
kingdoms and principalities of ice.
I mask, I camouflage your exposed face
Screening it from the scary visage of truth
Suddenly peering through an uncemented crack.

Call me a bloom-child, a flower
For I ruffle into bloom like a flower
Full of face and colour, turning to seed,
My footprints on paper.

Call me Most Powerful. Without me
No Holy Scripture, love, song, history.
Absolute, total, abysmal my hold over creatures,
Weaving webs of emotion, splashing in signature,

And the uncanny, eerie ability to breed
Drifts of dream, breed formations of thought.
Spellbinding, mesmerising, enthralling
This magical gift, this power.
Oh I send thought kerb-crawling
To the Gates of Anywhere!

The tongue is my fleshy stage, the platform where
I don the costume of my character
The tongue can no man tame – the tongue is a fire
Unruly evil full of deadly poison
I dance on tongues as on a trottoir
Oh I have known it capable of venom,
The robust, well-saliva'ed tongue which launches
Its death-bird into holocausting branches.

Mark this, mark this, mark this:
Toxins of astonishing virulence
Evolved by Chironex Fleckeri,
The Medusa Jelly-fish, as well as by
The highly venomous Taipan Snake of
The tubular fang (unprepossessing tongue –
flickering, forked)
Are being milked for secretions
Capable of modification into
Invaluable therapeutic substance:
Sincere milk of the word.
Strong salt of goodness.

MY WORD'S A SHEEPDOG

I did not realise I had a soul
until one late midsummer dusk, an owl
suddenly hung its smoky whiteness
above my head.
Not quite transparent, luminous and ghostly
softer than soft, not menacing, not swooping,
balanced above the cornfield
glowing in the air.

My Word's a sheepdog. I can see it scurry,
nipping the heels of thought, rounding it up
when it meanders into imprecision.
Calm down, calm down. Attentively together
let us try to retreat into abstraction.

In the beginning when I was created
I called God Father of Words, Omnipotent,
I would not dream to question
the rules of His grammar.
But here I break down. Thought's the wrong size.

The Escape

THE ROADS OF EUROPE

War winds wail over Europe
Stars fall and bodies fall
Give me a spade – let us die
The grave's a black hole.

A million refugees drag
Their bellies – babies – bags
Where will they anchor – where
Their lives – their rags?

Shapeless – untidy – bulky
String-tied the bundles they carry
Photograph-album – icon –
Kitten – canary –

Silently – painfully – slowly
Mile after mile after mile
They tread their way to gas ovens
Death-camps – exile.

Kyrie eleison – where is
The God they worshipped and feared
Who made and counted every hair
Of their heads and beards?

"I've seen it, seen it." . . . Absently
Filling in details
History stops to urinate
Bites grubby nails.

THEY ARE HARNESSING THE HORSES

They are harnessing the horses while I pack
Strapping the House the best I can firmly to my back

With no time for anything in the frantic hurry
Except essentialest essentials: here's the inventory:

Peasant song at harvesting – the forest of birds –
My little Notebook with book-titles and my Book of Words.

A star – a bee – a nightingale – several sunflower grains –
The clearest greenest stretch of river to lure down my veins –

Bunch of berries ripening on the mountain ash –
Choir of frogs – sound of one solitary splash –

Missal – feather of a stork – for luck a four-leaved clover
My Parker pen – the amber bead necklace from my lover –

Snowed up vision of a pine – crowing of the cock –
And the clock that's always late, my poor erratic clock.

Almost, almost left behind: scent of pine-tree cone
And the tiniest little chunk of my Polish moon.

THE PRAYER IN THE BARN

17th September, 1939

'How narrow the line which separates an adventure
from an ordeal and escape from exile.'
(Nicholson, of Byron's last journey.)

How fatalistic, the eternal mother, alone on deadly highroads
with her children, horses, their oats, their hay, the paper
money fit for the bonfire. Round them burning country. On
their heels the invader.

It rains when they leave the old ancestral house.
The dogs are held back.
Shouts of farewell. They do not really hear what the white
walls are saying. The poplars point West,
West, then North-West. The horses trot, amble, steam
through a barrage of leaves, mud, puddles, flooding,
the empty track, wet fields, streams without bridges,
marshy lane, swamp, deep ditches, valley of death.
Birches converge on them in startled groups,
astonishing their whiteness. The war wind
wails, whimpers, agitates – another victim
of some catastrophe, some awful grieving.
The road strains out towards frontiers.
And would she now turn back if someone told her:
"There's no returning. You are leaving for ever – "?

Like arteries down a leaf, disaster runs
deep in the blood of races too long exposed.
And now the children giggle in the straw.
This is adventure. Books have prepared them for this.

Later they stop. A barn. Wide open. Deserted.
They know they are surrounded. The weather thickens.
The horses urinate. The youngest child
Runs round the cart, whistles encouragement.
The straw holds golden gleams in the eerie light.

Is this then the beginning of the Great Persecution?
Who if she called would hear among the immortals?
She prays on the chaffy floor of the barn:

The seventeenth of September.
Europe blows out its lamps
Three children – six horses – myself
In the midst of enemy camps
O my children

Thirteen – sixteen – seventeen –
Is it for this I raised you
My poor fledglings?
Murder – rape – Siberia?
There is poison in my pocket.

Old Siwak snorts and neighs
Head lurching homewards.
Vast and heavy as Russia
An immense sadness weighs
Over the bedraggled potato fields.

Rescue us, holy Angel, rescue and heal,
I appeal to you not to hurt
The earth and the trees before you seal
The foreheads of the chosen
With the Sign

That guides through calamity.
The divine master-key.
May our foreheads shine
Not because of our merits, but
By the grace of those others

Before us: friends – uncles – mothers
Who lived justly, obeyed the commandments
Were good to neighbours.
You, who guided Tobias and his dog
(We left ours behind)

And with the gall of the fish healed the blind
Eyes of Tobit, smoking Satan out with
The burnt entrails of that fish.
Come to our help, holy Angel; I realise
You may not appear angelic – wear disguise.

It is then he appears, dismounts and offers help,
A priest in flight with the white Host,
Christ's body, the bread of angels.
His only luggage, this. The strange elopement!
Old cart. Brown horse. Tired man. Dog-collar. Dust.
He knows the way by heart and leads. They follow.
They do not recognise the Angel in him.

THE ABANDONED HOUSE

17th September, 1939

They have abandoned the House.
The abandoned House
Has no idea that it is for ever.
Has never practised gestures of farewell.
It stands bedraggled in the streaming air
And stoops supporting its uneven towers.
Around it trees on guard like green archangels.

Emptiness. Absence. Rain stampedes the roof.
A door half-open screeches.
The House is drawn to
Secretive stirrings on the painted floor:
The thin flat progress of the centipede,
Spider suspended in mid-air. Flies
Around the glass of milk, the half-peeled apple.

But listen – listen – listen: legs of tables
Chairs – mirrors – wooden surfaces converse
Quietly with each other, the chest of drawers,
The round muttering clock, the walking stick.
Bewildered the House listens intently,
Stares at the ceiling – no one here to counsel –
Steps back a little into earlier reasons
(Still audible the ruined reverberations):
Helena searches for the iodine
She needs it urgently for the young bull,
Ecstatic Zofia gallops round the lawn,
Jerzy, teenager, in his sailor suit
Reciting poetry. Shakes with emotion.
Andrew, the freckled-one gathering pears

Into a little Belorussian cap.
Olga with logs – Olga with chamberpots,
Pan Kuzian sings about a shining star
Which trembled at the moment of his birth, *
Ladies in summer frocks, Alek at the piano,
The dogs, each at his post, respecting each other.
The simple smells of baking from the kitchen . . .

Where gone the sound of footsteps?
Where gone the voices
And words – alive –
Running from mouth to mouth?

Silence. No movement.
A sudden freak of a leaf
Torn from the tree too early
Glues itself
Against the window pane of the dining room.
Rain on the hagberry. Rain on the poplars.
The scent of apples from the empty garden.

They have abandoned the House one hour before noon.
The inexplicable abandonment.

But who will feed the dogs
close – open – doors
water the horses
light the lamps at night
organise the sowing of oats
pay peoples' wages?

And will the walls shriek out
wooden floors creak

* O gwiazdeczko coś błyszczała gdym ja ujrzał świat.

and chairs and tables
under hostile hands?

How can a House protest?
Unhook its bats
Bite nails
hang down the head
bow stooping shoulders?

No answer. Silence.
Winds of disaffection
rising from Asia
announce the first looters.

THE HOUSE IS NOW SURROUNDED

The House is now surrounded by carts and horses
Broken, uneven line of arms and boots
Grey apparitions slithering in haste
Conspiratorial, cautious in scattered groups
They seem unsteady, drunken, but not with wine.
A cow moos nearby. The trees fill with rustling.

The House withdraws – recedes into the earth
Slaps them with emptiness. It is wide open.

So it begins: the plight of inanimate objects
Chair – table – carpet – clock – bed – pillow – sheet
Mattress and candle – picture – yellow sandal –
The round Venetian mirror – porcelain.

"Chadzi siuda – *psiakrew cholera* – shit –
Son of a bitch – bloodsuckin *sukin syn* –
Not a crumb in the mother-fucking drawer!"

Armfuls of clothing – curtain – strawberry
Raspberry jam – pickled cucumber – herring.
Kiełbasa – kwas – wool – cotton – only silk
Hisses in anger – swishes, growls, recoils.
Photograph album – tennis racket – chess
Saucepan and frying pan – inside them books
Book upon book – paper's good for burning.
A crystal vase splintering wounds the fingers.
Chewing at something sticky like a sweet
A blond youth pisses on the hollyhocks . . .

Poverty – anger – puzzlement – sweat – commotion
Grieving enormous stare of the House.

And will they ever find the buried silver
Guarded by moss and three boletus mushrooms?

Come, let us reconnoitre the looted Palace.
The two young peasant girls creep in on tiptoes
Not even daring to whisper. They've never stood
In anything so empty
A toothless mouth
Preparing for a shriek . . . splinters of glass
String – something bloody spilt
A broken chair – feathers – paper – torn –
A white page – on it the word HYACINTH.

Fugitive light – the floor escapes into shadows
Several grubby rags dance a black dance
Room after room after room.

A piano – look –
Why left behind?
Giant in mourning clothes
So absolutely mournful
Collapsed in a corner.

They stare troubled – do not understand
There is a mystery here – a waste – a pity
A hint of madness on the spooky floor
A grieving for the looters and the looted.

The howling of a dog. And suddenly
Bang – bang – bang – bang – bang – bang
The savage roaring
From the black piano in the empty room.
A bomb? A thunderbolt? Some awful haunting?
Shriek of the toothless mouth held in until now?

WHY DO I FEEL INDIFFERENT?

Why do I feel indifferent
About the sacking of the House?
Is it because the shock is blurred
By half a century of Time?
Because I know the House is gone
Like a wild creature into earth?
Because the drums of history
Deep in the marrow of the bone
Insist it is impossible
To lead a human life of peace
On the flat parapets of Russia?

Was I too young to be attached
To even beautiful furniture?
Too thoughtless to grieve at the loss
Of a beloved chest of drawers?

It is the dog who breaks my heart
Bewildered on the kitchen floor
And was he spared by the looters?
I do not know I do not know
We should have killed him before we left.

I watch them drag their loot their feet
And will they have the wisdom to
Divide it all between themselves?
Poor everlasting looters, who
Will find so little' gold in cofre'
And not enough to make them rich.

EXILE

Shaking the fist of the heart
Straight as the crow flies home
Dream back swallowed-up country
Scratch into surface soil
From sundered earth lift up
Ripened against the tanks
The childhood acre

You've heard it
Heard it all
The crime-crossed borders
The bankrupt currency
The brace of babies
To reach and rest
With room to keep
Sleep in
Whitewashed belonging room
To spread wings in and sign
Not on the dotted line
Give birth to a new passport

Yet the further you get away
Safe – with your tumbledown trunks –
The stranger the foreign sea
The sadder the siren sings.

NOT ON THE TOURIST ROUTE

'If in planting a coffee tree you bend the tap-root the tree will start after a little time to put out a multitude of small delicate roots near the surface. That tree will never thrive nor bear fruit but it will flower more richly than the others. The fine roots are the dreams of the tree. As it puts them out it need no longer think of its bent tap-root.

Isak Dinesen

Wisely dryly of roots and loss you ramble on
in your outlandish accent upsetting the tee-aitches.
Dryly wisely of loss and uprooting in strictly
biological terms, when – snap – all of a sudden
the acquired upper lip – strip of narrow elastic collapses into
red hot emotional talk – foreigner that you are –
magnet for misery, oh, brandishing before the
embarrassed all and sundry the naked spectacle of
a fury of roots – stem, tendril and all –
unseemly – bulky – raw – awkward parsnip affair
to pull out of anywhere –
with – left behind – huge chunks.
How many? Count them – count –
How many? Two at least? Fangs of the mammal beast
absently left to rot in long ago garden
with other paraphernalia.
Not on the tourist route.

THREE GRAVES

Three graves on a hill
Where larches rooted
The war broke out
The law broke down
The vultures hooted
The armies came
The armies went
The graves were looted.

MY TWO COUNTRIES

With anguish and with anger I look back
Upon the awful flatness of my first country
Perilous flatness that made it defenceless

Generous flatness – proud and trusting flatness
Reckless snowdrifty death-defying flatness
Unfenced and gullible – perishing for ever.

And then the way it shrank and atrophied
Squeezed in and out of borders – allowing maps
To play their cruel hokey-pokey games.

Away from flatness then I pitched the tent
Of my adopted land – on the granite rock
Top of a Celtic hill. A tidal sea

Keeps out invading hordes. The pebbles give
A sound of hissing with the sea's withdrawal.
I fill my eyes with seabirds and shapes of boats.

And there are whiffs of magic here. Listen
Be still and listen: small stampede of hooves
The hooves of unicorns – a muffled sound.

Envoi

THE WORD HAS A SEVERE NOSE-BLEED

Epistaxis

Word is having a nose-bleed – the first of a lifetime.
Instructed by kind GPs he pinches the nose
tightly below the bridge – leans eagerly forward
over the deep tin bowl on the kitchen table.
The sound of blood is the sound of muffled drums.

Forbidden nostrils, blood opts for the throat
Splutters and oozes and drips with uncanny abandon
Along the folds of tongue rolled out like a carpet.
The red uncloistered drops astonish the air.
The nose – that trusted ally – has become a leaky
Tap – unreliable – no longer a Sniffer.

Embarrassed baffled Word searches round for a joke.
Fare bella figura appears important . . .

Arterial now, deliberate, volcanic and pensive
The blood coagulates inside the bowl
Into a wobbly quivering blackberry coloured
Primordial *kisiel* – dessert reminiscent of childhood.

Language is blood – blood language –
How much can I spare
Out of my ration of eight full pints?
In a panic
Word recognises now the bodies of letters
A – B – C – D – S – Z – the exhausted phonemes –
The arm – the leg – the head – their drowning splash –
Their jellied thickenings – their bloody cocoonings –
Falling apart – dissolving – agonising – spilling –
Each dragging ancient trusted umbilical meanings . . .

My lymph – my sap – my life-blood –
My wedded language –
My heritage – my first identity –
Transfusion – anaemia – loss –
Word collapses
Wrapped up in cellular blankets
Carried out on a stretcher.

BLOOD TRANSFUSION

Shivering on the hospital bed Word remembers
the torrents of lost blood with tenderness
but oh how strange how strange
and rather disgusting
that it should so depart without a farewell!
The shock is hard to bear and Word is stricken
watches the creeping pallor in fingers and toes
all the time trying not to agonise
over the draughty shrieks of depleted veins.

"We cannot let you perish from a nose-bleed."
Adroitly the Nurse
punctures a patch of arm and hooks on to it
intricate coils of tubing descending from
a BAG OF BLOOD – flat – blackish – tightly packed
and like a dwarfish udder with four teats.
From this anonymous plastic plasma drips.

This then is the Great Invasion.
Word is aware
of strong strange fluids entering the body
alien corpuscles knocking at the veins.
They know how to read the map, they navigate
up and down vessels, trunk road, arteries
pushed right left right left right
by the pump of the heart
to rest the soles of their feet
against the aorta . . .

Is this then the NEW LANGUAGE pouring in?
Sea letters – island letters – Viking letters –
Celtic – Teutonic – Druid – Anglo-Saxon –
bawdy – Shakespearean – metaphysical . . .

Outnumbered – the Slavonic entities
hang down their head.
ousted by BLOOD is *KREW*.

Has something extraordinary happened?
Word's apprehensive
unable to pinpoint
the exact nature of the transmutation.
A loss? A gain?
Each untranslatable.

The precious liquid flows
whatever its name.

HAIKUS FROM HOSPITAL

Symptoms of trouble
Stomach – a blown-up balloon
Weight loss, belly ache.

For days on end now
Like a tin drum the stomach
That's what's wrong with me.

Cancer is announced
Silently enters the great
Executioner.

Cancer is announced
Suddenly the Kingdom of God
Seems around the corner.

Ah but I shall miss
Krysia the loveliest daughter
And several friends.

I reach rock bottom
Ask the nurse, "Am I dying?"
She answers "You're not."

Dr Christopher Rickford –
Gesture of farewell –
Gently squeezes toes.

Tricky to swallow
Each gulp a marathon
Tricky to survive.

"Please buy my warts."
I said to my brother
"One penny each," he said.

Now I know
I shall not live to a hundred
Something I dreaded.

I TALK TO MY CANCER

I talk to my cancer a lot.
Cancer, Cancer, what is this plot
to oust me from the land of living?

Enigmatic insidious
grazing on me – and ox on grass –
I imagine you spawning spawning
thousand cells – asymmetrical pink
in each cell bloated eye – black as ink –
abstract painting by Salvadore Dali . . .

Cancer, cancer, I deeply resent
this intrusion without my consent
brute – invader – parasite – squatter –
having forced me to dance more or less
on the tightrope between life and death
condemning me now for that matter
to this battle, this duel for life
chemotherapy – discipline – prayer –
mental use of my little black knife,
cleansing floods of luminous water
to flush out your mysterious power . . .

Du calme, o my soul – easy – easy
carcinomas are not for sissies . . .

Praise your enemies if they deserve
your respect. Praise your adversary.
Cancer, though I admit you have
half-demolished my house – can you be
some astonishing messenger from
worlds as yet not open to me?
For since you called – unforeseen

gifts are showered. How else to explain
clearness in the meaning of things
God – dream – vision – eternal city –
joy – hope – quietness – infinity
Cancer, cancer, do you hold the key?

Cancer does not answer.